INTERMEDIATE PIANO DUET

1 PIANO, 4 HANDS

HYMN ✠ FAVORITES

Arranged by Larry Moore

CONTENTS

ISBN-13: 978-1-4234-4924-9
ISBN-10: 1-4234-4924-X

HAL•LEONARD®
CORPORATION
7777 W. BLUEMOUND RD. P.O. BOX 13819 MILWAUKEE, WI 53213

In Australia Contact:
Hal Leonard Australia Pty. Ltd.
4 Lentara Court
Cheltenham, Victoria, 3192 Australia
Email: ausadmin@halleonard.com.au

Visit Hal Leonard Online at
www.halleonard.com

ABIDE WITH ME

SECONDO

Words by HENRY F. LYTE
Music by WILLIAM H. MONK

ABIDE WITH ME

PRIMO

Words by HENRY F. LYTE
Music by WILLIAM H. MONK

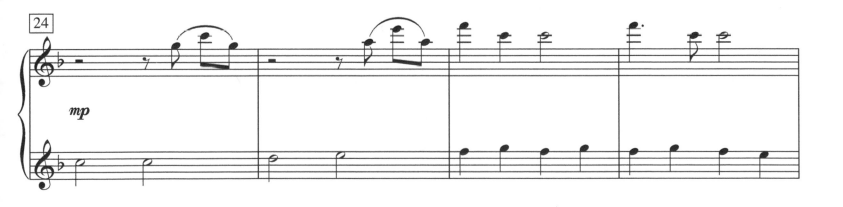

SECONDO

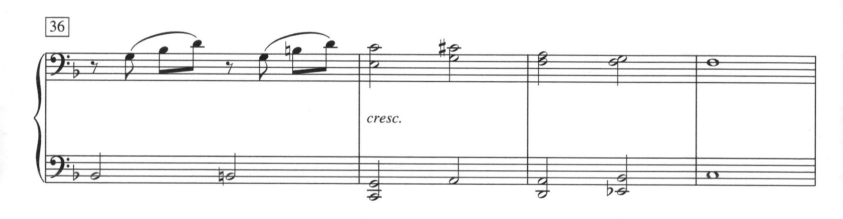

8vb

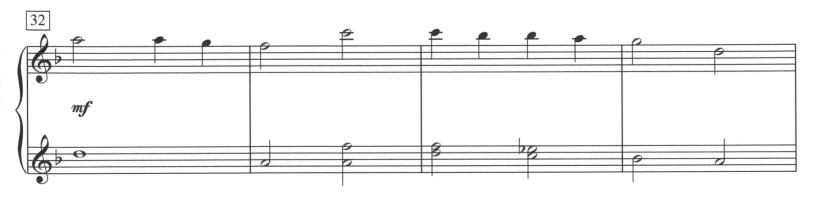

BEAUTIFUL SAVIOR

SECONDO

Words from *Munsterisch Gesangbuch*
Translated by JOSEPH A. SEISS
Music adapted from Silesian Folk Tune

BEAUTIFUL SAVIOR

PRIMO

Words from *Munsterisch Gesangbuch*
Translated by JOSEPH A. SEISS
Music adapted from Silesian Folk Tune

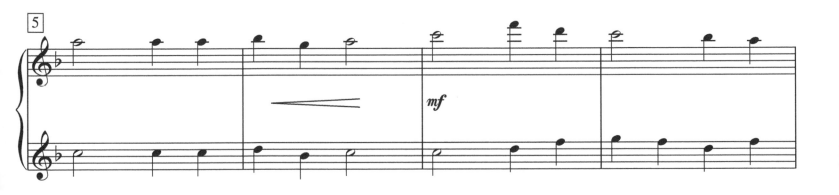

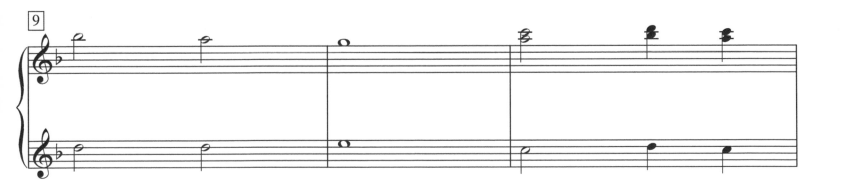

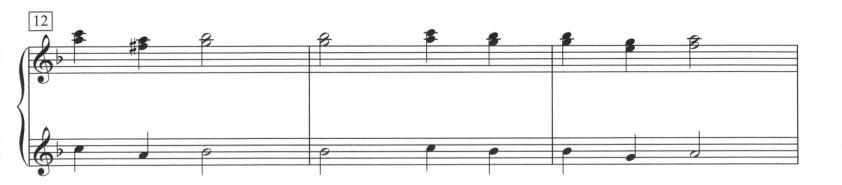

SECONDO

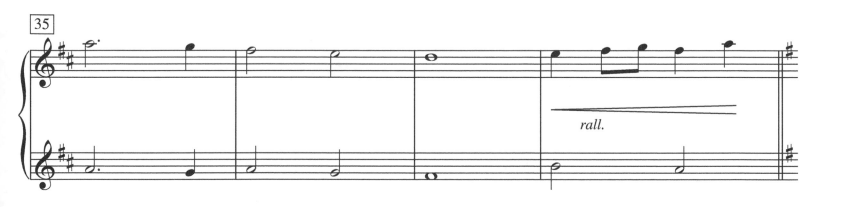

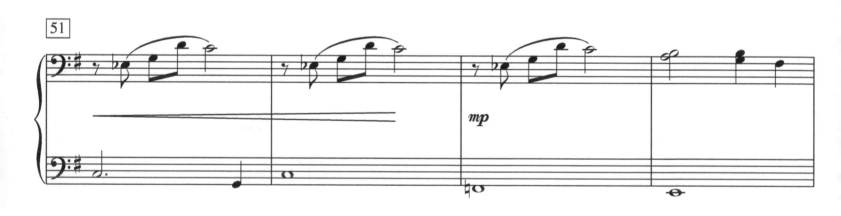

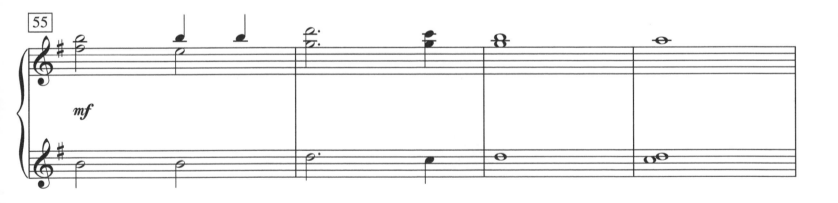

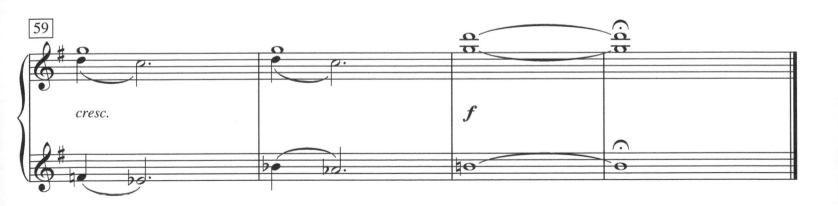

BLESSED ASSURANCE

SECONDO

Lyrics by FANNY J. CROSBY
Music by PHOEBE PALMER KNAPP

Flowing

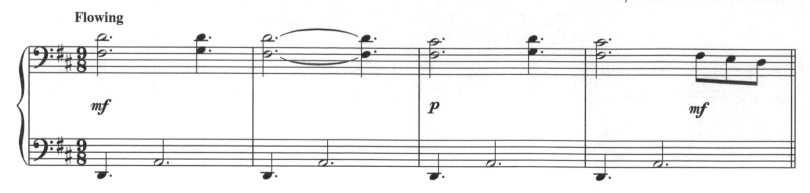

BLESSED ASSURANCE

PRIMO

Lyrics by FANNY J. CROSBY
Music by PHOEBE PALMER KNAPP

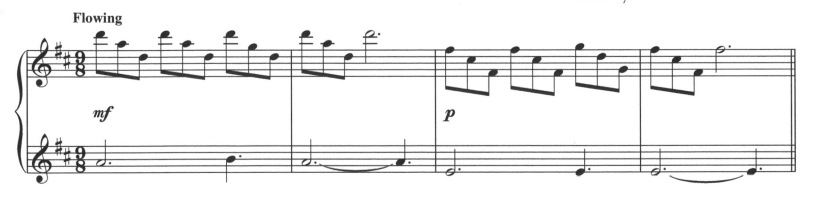

SECONDO

PRIMO

SECONDO

FAITH OF OUR FATHERS

SECONDO

Words by FREDERICK WILLIAM FABER
Music by HENRI F. HEMY and JAMES G. WALTON

Moderately

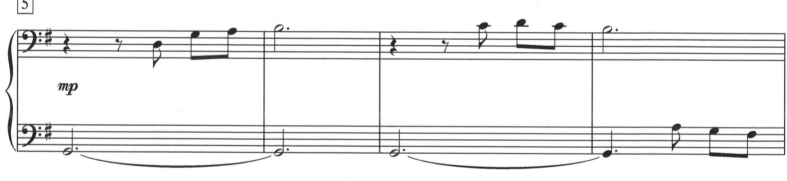

FAITH OF OUR FATHERS

PRIMO

Words by FREDERICK WILLIAM FABER
Music by HENRI F. HEMY and JAMES G. WALTON

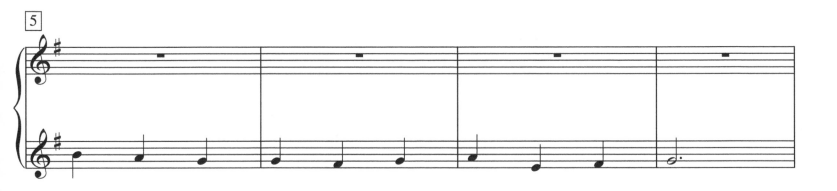

SECONDO

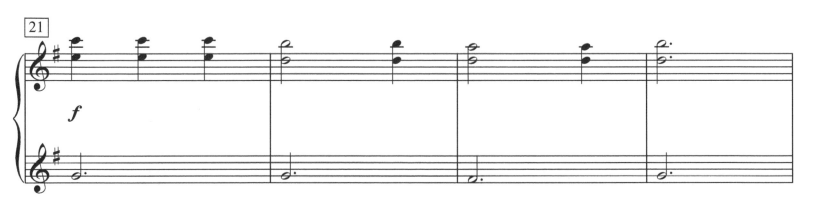

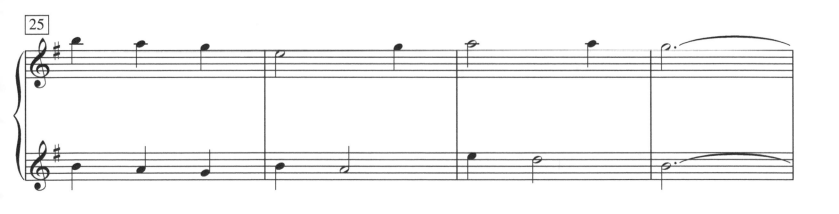

SECONDO

SECONDO

PRIMO

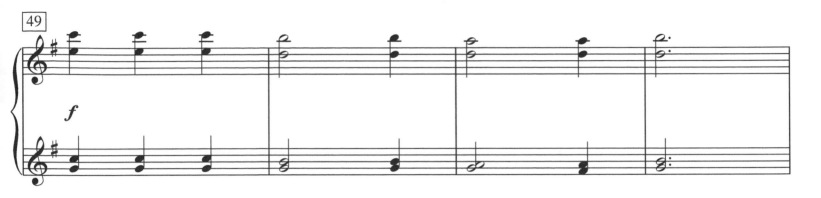

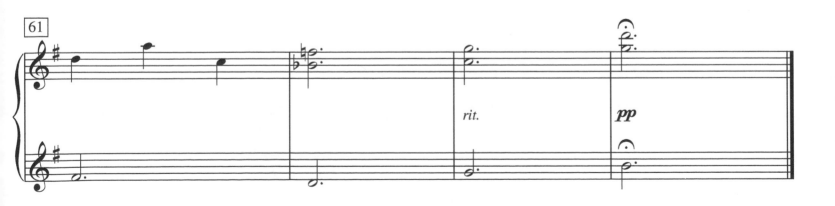

IN THE GARDEN

SECONDO

Words and Music by
C. AUSTIN MILES

Country Waltz

IN THE GARDEN

PRIMO

Words and Music by
C. AUSTIN MILES

SECONDO

SECONDO

PRIMO

MY FAITH LOOKS UP TO THEE

SECONDO

Words by RAY PALMER
Music by LOWELL MASON

MY FAITH LOOKS UP TO THEE

PRIMO

Words by RAY PALMER
Music by LOWELL MASON

SECONDO

PRIMO

40

SECONDO

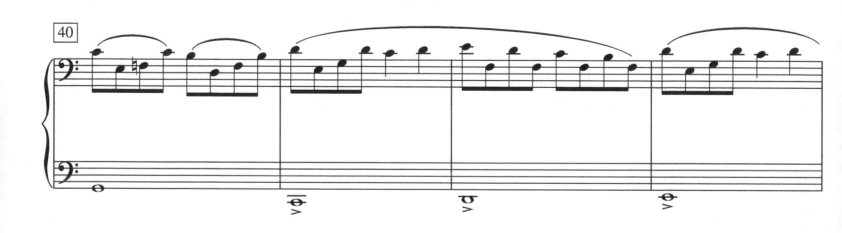

PRIMO

NEARER, MY GOD, TO THEE

SECONDO

Words by SARAH F. ADAMS
Based on Genesis 28:10-22
Music by LOWELL MASON

NEARER, MY GOD, TO THEE

PRIMO

Words by SARAH F. ADAMS
Based on Genesis 28:10-22
Music by LOWELL MASON

SECONDO

PRIMO

THE OLD RUGGED CROSS

SECONDO

Words and Music by
REV. GEORGE BENNARD

THE OLD RUGGED CROSS

PRIMO

Words and Music by
REV. GEORGE BENNARD

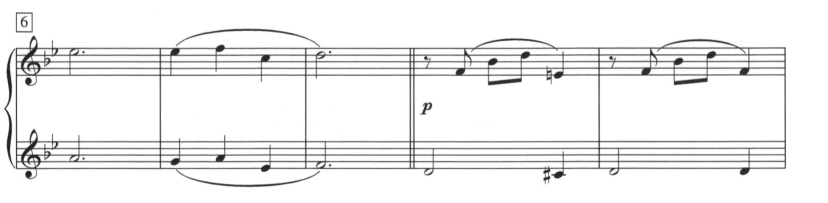

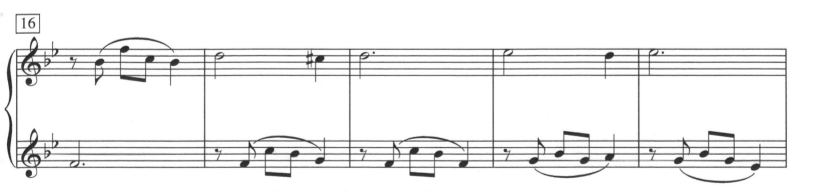

SECONDO

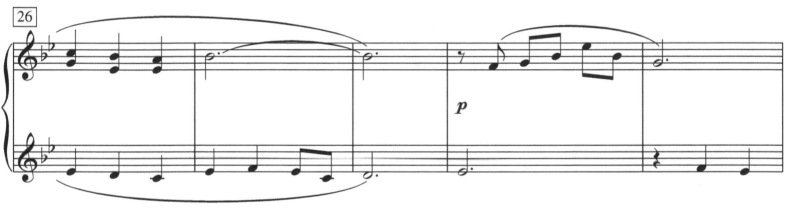

SECONDO

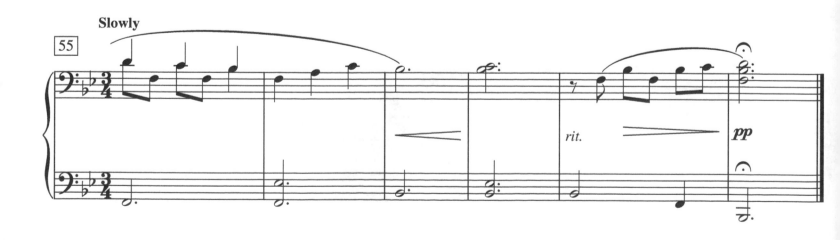

PRIMO

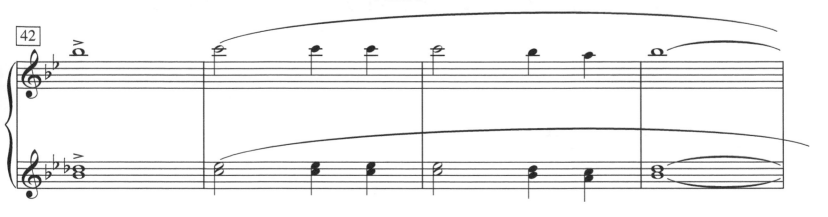

ONWARD, CHRISTIAN SOLDIERS

SECONDO

Words by SABINE BARING-GOULD
Music by ARTHUR S. SULLIVAN

March tempo

ONWARD, CHRISTIAN SOLDIERS

PRIMO

Words by SABINE BARING-GOULD
Music by ARTHUR S. SULLIVAN

Majestically

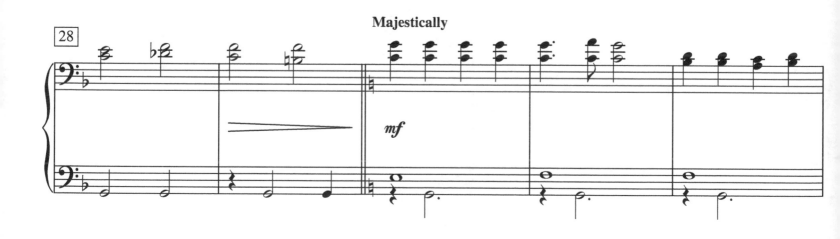

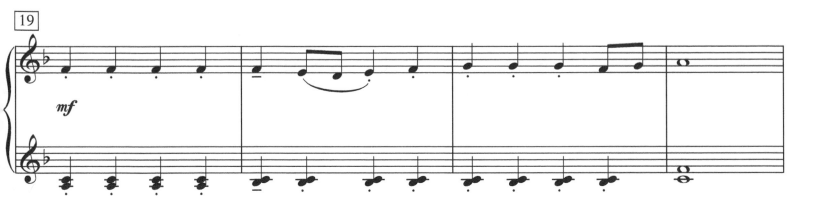

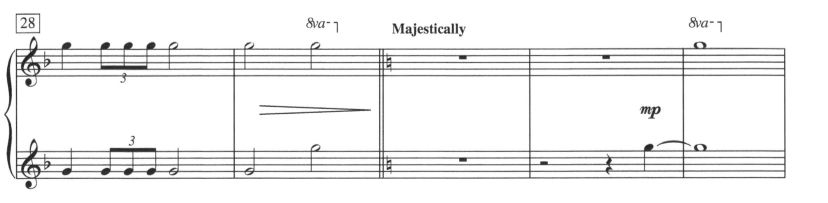

SECONDO

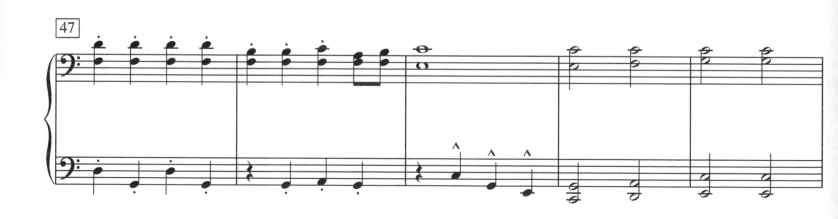

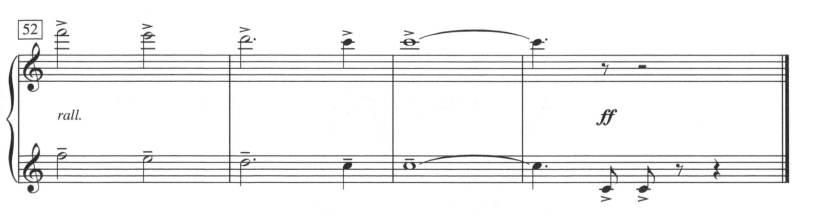

ROCK OF AGES

SECONDO

Words by AUGUSTUS M. TOPLADY
Music by THOMAS HASTINGS

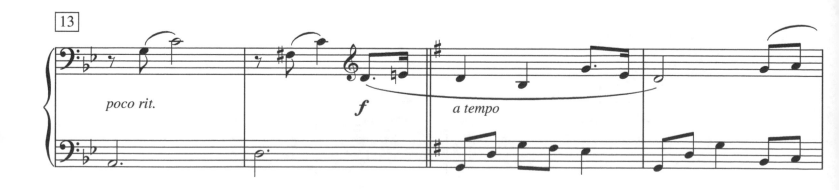

ROCK OF AGES

PRIMO

Words by AUGUSTUS M. TOPLADY
Music by THOMAS HASTINGS

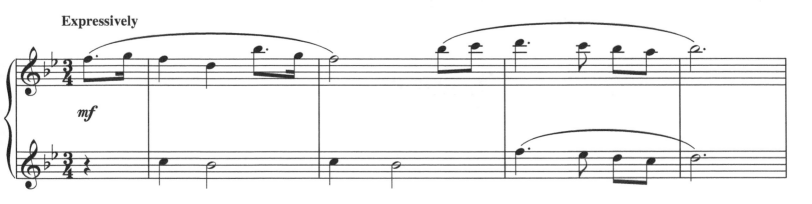

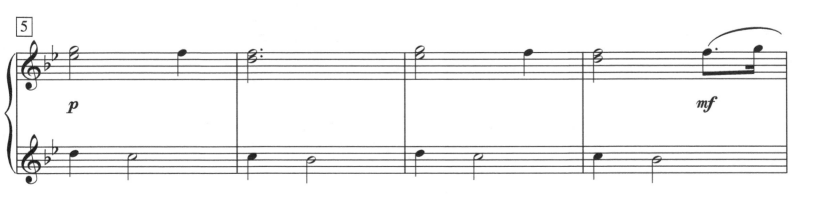

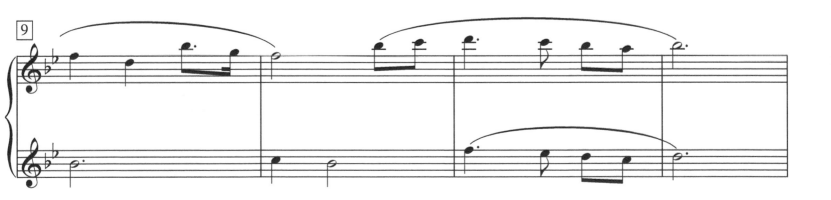

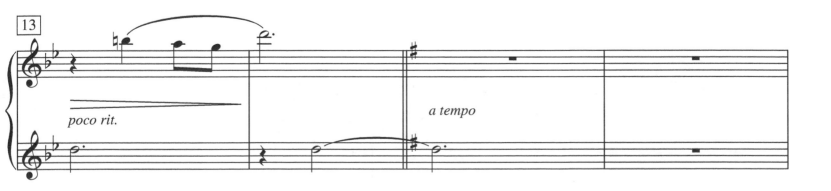

SECONDO

PRIMO

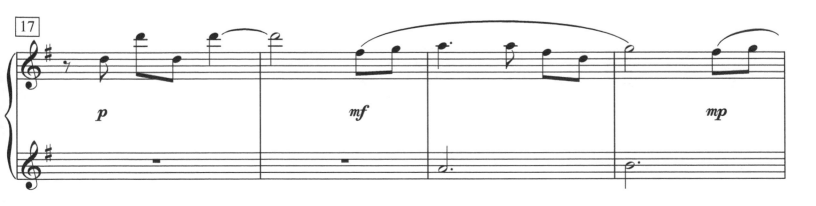

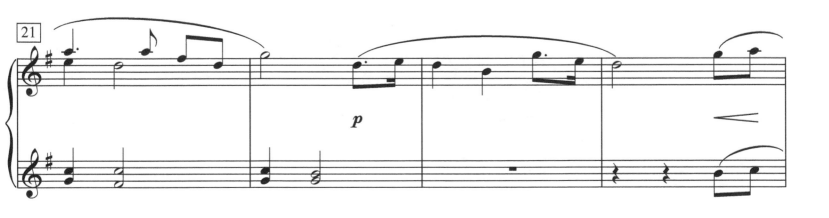

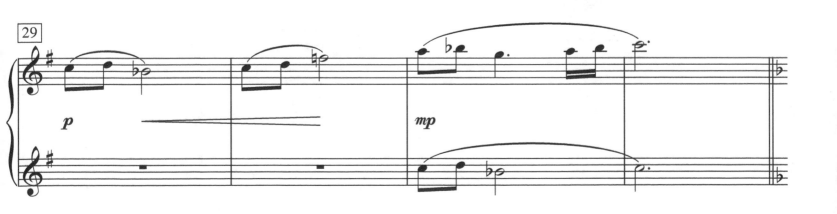

SECONDO

STAND UP, STAND UP FOR JESUS

SECONDO

Words by GEORGE DUFFIELD, JR.
Music by GEORGE J. WEBB

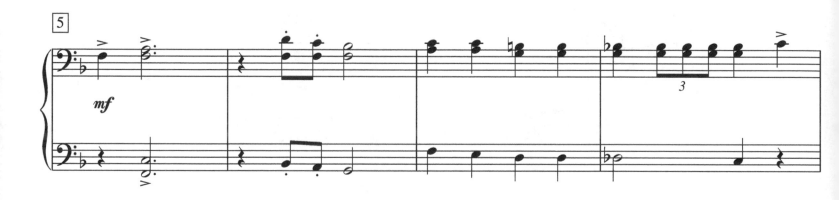

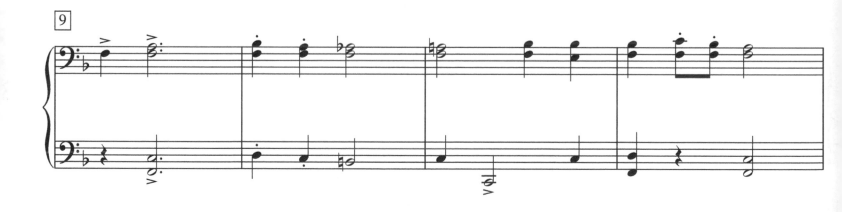

STAND UP, STAND UP FOR JESUS

PRIMO

Words by GEORGE DUFFIELD, JR.
Music by GEORGE J. WEBB

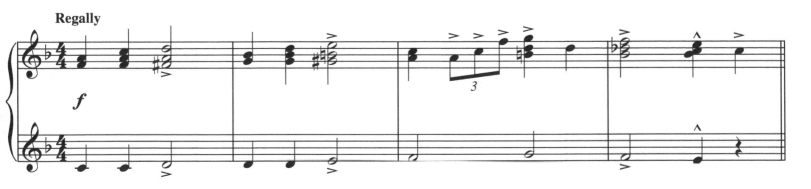

SECONDO

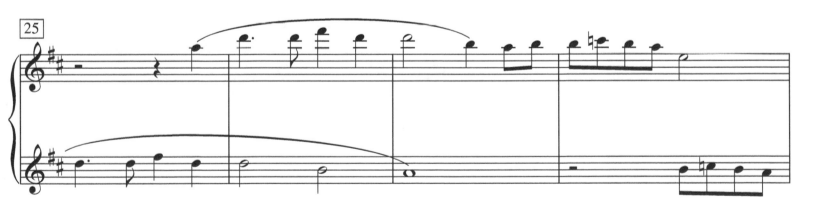

SECONDO

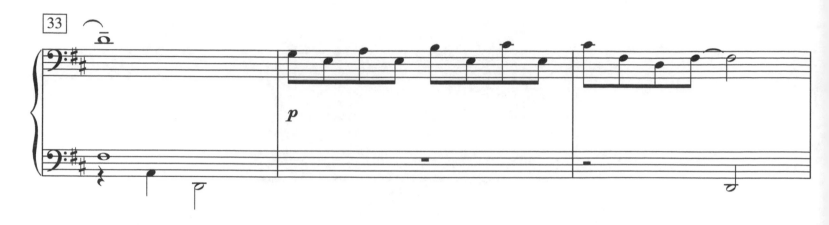

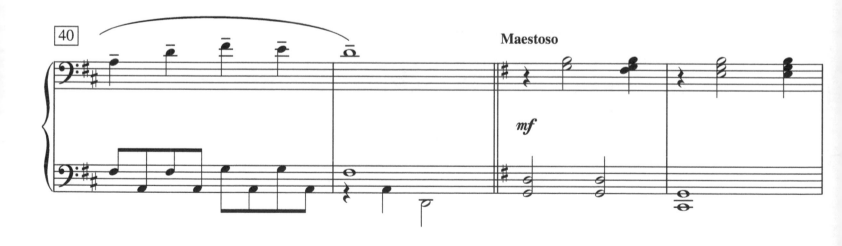

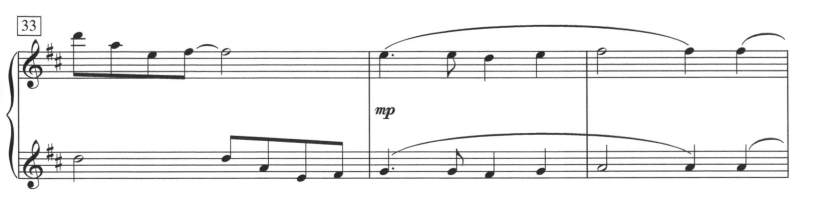

SECONDO

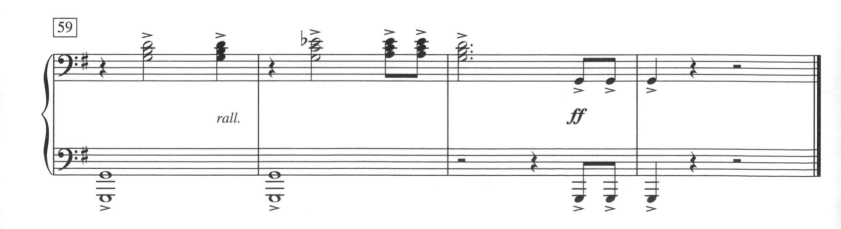

WE GATHER TOGETHER

SECONDO

Words from *Nederlandtsch Gedenckclanck*
Translated by THEODORE BAKER
Netherlands Folk Melody

Moderately

p cantabile

mp

WE GATHER TOGETHER

PRIMO

Words from *Nederlandtsch Gedenckclanck*
Translated by THEODORE BAKER
Netherlands Folk Melody

SECONDO

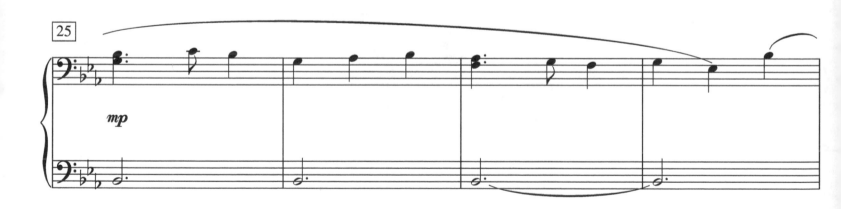

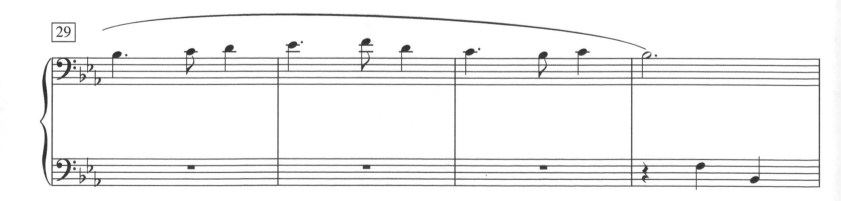

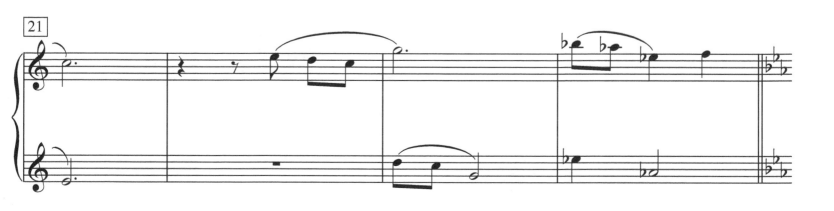

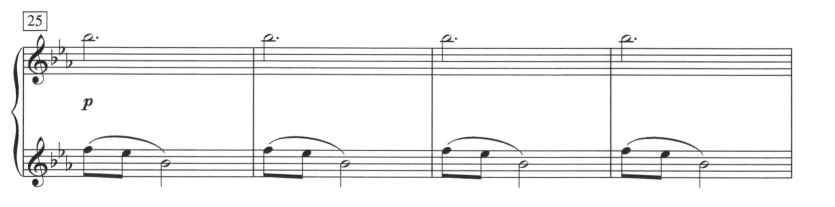

SECONDO

SECONDO

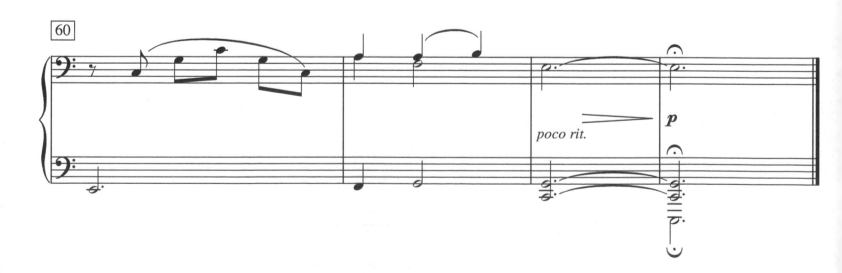

PRIMO

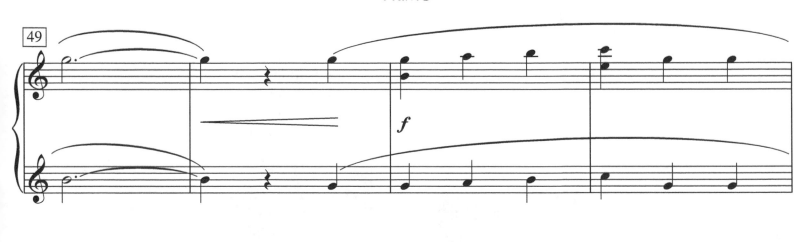

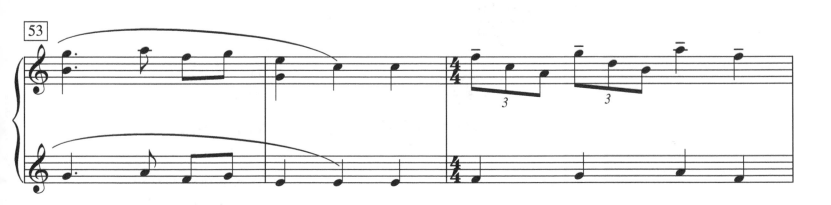

PIANO DUETS

The **Piano Duet Play-Along** series is an excellent source for 1 piano, 4 hand duets in every genre! It also gives you the flexibility to rehearse or perform piano duets anytime, anywhere! Play these delightful tunes with a partner, or use the accompanying audio to play along with either the Secondo or Primo part on your own. The audio files are enhanced so performers can adjust the recording to any tempo without changing pitch.

1. Piano Favorites
00290546 Book/CD Pack $14.95

2. Movie Favorites
00290547 Book/CD Pack $14.95

3. Broadway for Two
00290548 Book/CD Pack $14.95

4. The Music of Andrew Lloyd Webber™
00290549 Book/CD Pack $14.95

5. Disney Favorites
00290550 Book/CD Pack $14.95

6. Disney Songs
00290551 Book/CD Pack $14.95

7. Classical Music
00290552 Book/CD Pack $14.95

8. Christmas Classics
00290554 Book/CD Pack $14.95

9. Hymns
00290556 Book/CD Pack $14.95

10. The Sound of Music
00290557 Book/CD Pack $17.99

11. Disney Early Favorites
00290558 Book/CD Pack $16.95

12. Disney Movie Songs
00290559 Book/Online Audio $16.99

13. Movie Hits
00290560 Book/CD Pack $14.95

14. Les Misérables
00290561 Book/CD Pack $16.95

15. God Bless America® & Other Songs for a Better Nation
00290562 Book/CD Pack $14.99

16. Disney Classics
00290563 Book/CD Pack $16.95

19. Pirates of the Caribbean
00290566 Book/CD Pack $16.95

20. Wicked
00290567 Book/CD Pack $16.99

21. Peanuts®
00290568 Book/CD Pack $16.99

22. Rodgers & Hammerstein
00290569 Book/CD Pack $14.99

23. Cole Porter
00290570 Book/CD Pack $14.99

24. Christmas Carols
00290571 Book/CD Pack $14.95

25. Wedding Songs
00290572 Book/CD Pack $14.99

26. Love Songs
00290573 Book/CD Pack $14.99

27. Romantic Favorites
00290574 Book/CD Pack $14.99

28. Classical for Two
00290575 Book/CD Pack $14.99

29. Broadway Classics
00290576 Book/CD Pack $14.99

30. Jazz Standards
00290577 Book/CD Pack $14.99

31. Pride and Prejudice
00290578 Book/CD Pack $14.99

32. Sondheim for Two
00290579 Book/CD Pack $16.99

33. Twilight
00290580 Book/CD Pack $14.99

36. Holiday Favorites
00290583 Book/CD Pack $14.99

37. Christmas for Two
00290584 Book/CD Pack $14.99

38. Lennon & McCartney Favorites
00290585 Book/CD Pack $14.99

39. Lennon & McCartney Hits
00290586 Book/CD Pack $14.99

40. Classical Themes
00290588 Book/Online Audio $14.99

41. The Phantom of the Opera
00290589 Book/CD Pack $16.99

42. Glee
00290590 Book/CD Pack $16.99

43. A Merry Little Christmas
00102044 Book/CD Pack $14.99

44. Frozen
00128260 Book/Online Audio $14.99

45. Coldplay
00141054 Book/Online Audio $14.99

View complete songlists at
Hal Leonard Online at **www.halleonard.com**

Disney characters and artwork are © Disney Enterprises, Inc.

1116